WHAT WE FAIL

TO REALIZE — Vol. I

by Anthony J. Fryer (Smiley)

OPENING LETTER

Dear Reader,

I appreciate you.

This book was never meant to be perfect—neither are we. It was written through reflection, pain, faith, and a desire to grow beyond my own limitations. Every word here is a reminder that transformation begins the moment you stop hiding from yourself and start paying attention to the truth that has been calling your name.

This book was not born from comfort, but from growth I did not see coming.
There were nights I questioned everything — my worth, my path, even my purpose. Yet each time I rose, something stronger in me manifested.

I began writing this back in 2019 — the first and last time I was locked up. That moment gave me the silence and space I needed to see myself clearly for the first time.
Since then, I've learned to see my experiences differently — to find the good within what once felt like pain. Years later I ended up breaking mentally from taking tolls overtime, and I had a big epiphany — I know I am here for more than I can imagine.

I have learned that peace and ambition do not compete — they coexist when you learn to move with intention.
Awareness is the awakening. Perspective is the mirror. Mindset is the architect.
And through it all, the journey toward purpose is not about becoming someone new—it is about remembering who you already are.

As you move through these pages, take your time. Pause where you feel resistance. Reflect when something stirs your spirit. Some pages will speak softly; others might challenge you. But each one carries a piece of my experience and a reflection of yours.

If you take anything from this work, let it be the understanding that you have the power to redefine your life. No matter what you have faced or lost, no moment has been wasted. Everything has prepared you for this one.

Take a breath. Read slowly. This is not a race — it is a return.

Welcome to the process.

Thank you for trusting me with your time, your thoughts, and your energy.
May this serve as both a mirror and a map for your journey ahead.

With great purpose and infinite gratitude — my conviction is yours.

— Anthony J. Fryer largely known as Smiley

Dedication

For those who have fallen, risen, and are still climbing —

this book is for you.

For the ones who have been misunderstood, overlooked, or broken down by life,

yet somehow still chose to keep going.

For the silent believers who carry faith when no one is watching,

and for the version of myself who first picked up the pen back in 2019,

not knowing this moment would come.

May these words remind you that healing is not about perfection —

it is about returning to yourself.

Table of Contents

Closing Sections

Chapter 1

Awareness: Waking Up to Your Reality

Awareness & Perspective

We all experience moments when life becomes blurry. Clarity does not always arrive on time — sometimes truth reveals itself quietly. Awareness is not about perfection; it is about remembering. Perspective transforms pain into purpose. And when we return to awareness, everything realigns.

PRESENCE

"Cherish each day with all your being. Tomorrow is never promised. And if tomorrow arrives, it is still today."

INSIGHT:

> One moment, a person can be present, and the next, they are gone forever. It is always the one you least expect to meet death or perhaps, in the end it is truly life.
>
> Presence sharpens gratitude. When we detach from autopilot, we notice who and what we normally overlook. Loss is life's most effective reminder. Presence protects peace.

REFLECTION:

- Who deserves more presence from you today?
- What moment did you rush through recently?
- Where can you slow down right now?

LOVE & TIME

"Love is a profound experience that can be both painful and transformative. It is not a flawless entity and should not be forced or coerced. Instead, it should unfold naturally and organically. True love will eventually reveal itself, overcoming any obstacles that may arise."

INSIGHT:

> I am deeply in love, and I find myself constantly thinking about it throughout the day. Do you absolutely love someone? While I may believe it, only time will give the definitive answer.
>
> Love weakens when rushed and strengthens when experienced. Time clarifies sincerity. Forced affection is rooted in fear, authentic love rests in patience.

REFLECTION:

- Where are you forcing an outcome?
- What has time already revealed to you?
- What does healthy connection feel like?

GROWTH THROUGH UNITY

"Increased collaboration among individuals fosters collective growth and development. At this juncture, individuals attain a state of unity."

INSIGHT:

> Isolation can make you feel strong, but alignment makes you powerful. Growth multiplies when you stand with others who elevate your thinking, your discipline, and your vision.

REFLECTION:

- Who around you helps you grow — and who keeps you stagnant?
- What collaboration opportunity have you been avoiding out of pride or fear?

CHANGE BEGINS WITH YOU

"Change resides within you, not in the ability to impose it upon others. Over time, change may or may not materialize. However, by transforming yourself, you have the potential to influence the situations and circumstances surrounding you."

INSIGHT:

> Trying to change the world will drain you. Changing yourself influences everything the world puts in front of you. Shift your inner state and your outer life will eventually match it.

REFLECTION:

- Where have you been waiting for others to change before you move?
- What internal shift could change your outer experience right now?

POSITIVE MULTIPLICATION

"Positive times a Negative is equal to a Negative; Negative times a Negative is equal to a Negative; Positive times Positive equals a Positive."

Meaning:

"Positivity fosters positive alignment. Even on my most challenging days, I mentally prepared myself for a positive outlook."

INSIGHT:

Your mind is always multiplying. Positivity is not pretending — it is positioning. What you multiply inside eventually shows up outside.

REFLECTION:

- What thought have you been multiplying lately — positive or negative?
- How would your day shift if you made positivity a discipline instead of a mood?

DAILY ELEVATION

"Cultivate a positive mindset and consistently engage in self-improvement to foster a sense of well-being. Each day presents an opportunity for growth and enhancement."

INSIGHT:

Repetition builds reality. The smallest upgrades today lead to the largest breakthroughs tomorrow.

REFLECTION:

- What is one small improvement you can commit to today?
- When were you most consistent in your life? How did it feel?

SELF-RENEWAL

"Strive to be a better version of yourself today, than you ever were yesterday or before."

INSIGHT:

Improvement is not an event — it is a lifestyle. If you are not becoming more, you are settling for less.

REFLECTION:

- What part of yourself needs improvement right now?
- What small action today makes you better than yesterday?

MASTERY THROUGH CHALLENGE

"Overcoming challenges often requires simplicity, while pursuing the easier path can become more intricate."

INSIGHT:

> Life does not get easier — you get stronger. Hard choices create simple futures. Easy shortcuts create complicated consequences.

REFLECTION:

- What challenge are you avoiding because it's uncomfortable?
- Where have shortcuts created delays or setbacks?

HUNGER & BATTLE

"A warrior is almost always hungry and thirsty during battle, but a warrior cannot take a break to do so!"

INSIGHT:

> Discomfort does not mean defeat. True warriors learn to fight while hungry, tired, and tested.

REFLECTION:

- Where are you currently fighting a silent battle?
- What strength have you gained from not quitting?

STUDY AS A MINDSET

"I am actively engaged in my studies."

INSIGHT:

Study is not always school — it is awareness. Every day tests you. Every moment teaches you. When you study life, life reveals itself.

REFLECTION:

- What lesson has life taught you recently?
- Where can you observe instead of react?

UNCERTAINTY

"I prefer the certainty of death over the uncertainty of life. Assumptions can be detrimental, leading to stress, anger, confusion, and irritation. These negative emotions can only result in destructive behavior."

INSIGHT:

When you feel overwhelmed, do not give up. There will always be individuals facing greater challenges than you.

Assumptions shape emotional chaos. When clarity lacks, fear fills the gaps. Uncertainty invites curiosity, not surrender.

REFLECTION:

- What assumption is hurting you right now?
- How can you replace fear with patience?
- What can you ask for clarity on today?

END-OF-CHAPTER CHALLENGE

For the next 72 hours:

1. Practice slowing down intentionally.
2. Ask questions before assuming.
3. Choose patience when emotion rises.

Progress begins with awareness.

A.J.F.

Chapter 2

Perspective: The Lens That Shapes Your Life

Mindset & Inner Discipline

Mindset is not noise — it is navigation. Your thoughts become your habits. Your habits become your identity. A disciplined mind creates a disciplined life.

DISSONANCE

"Reevaluating one's life is crucial for determining one's path and actions. Repeating the same actions with the expectation of different outcomes is irrational."

INSIGHT:

Embrace change and maintain your authentic self. Strive to be the best version of yourself. What is your current plan?

Growth requires self-audit. When patterns stagnate, so do results. Perspective evolves when honesty increases.

REFLECTION:

- Where are you repeating instead of improving?
- Which version of you needs updating today?
- What habit no longer belongs?

NO LIMITS — ONLY BELIEF

"'Thug life' is a term used with pride to describe an individual who, despite humble beginnings, has achieved remarkable success through their own efforts.' (Also an acronym for The Hate U Give)" — Unknown Source

INSIGHT:

> Greatness is rarely born in comfort — it is forged in struggle, misunderstanding, and grit. Your starting place is never your final form unless you stay there.

REFLECTION:

- What hardship shaped your strength the most?
- Where have you underestimated your own rise?

ALIGNMENT OVER EVERYTHING

"God did not create us with a governor; rather, God created us with limitless potential!" — Linnea Blizzard

INSIGHT:

> Limitations are illusions built from fear, doubt, and conditioning. You were designed for expansion — but only you can unlock the door.

REFLECTION:

- Where are you still playing small?
- What part of your life needs faith over fear?

TRUE WEALTH BEGINS WITHIN

"Before you can make life-changing money, you need to, first, change your life." — Micah Walls

INSIGHT:

A rich mind builds a rich life. When your inner world evolves, your outer world responds.

REFLECTION:

- What habit holds you back from wealth?
- What mindset shift would change everything for you?

UNLIMITED GROWTH

"Mastery of all is attainable through the cultivation of learning."

INSIGHT:

Learning is not school — it is survival. Curiosity builds kings. Ignorance builds limits.

REFLECTION:

- What skill would transform your future if you mastered it?
- Are you consuming information or practicing wisdom?

HOPE VS. ACTION

"To hope or to attempt something is questionable thinking. We often fear the potential for failure rather than acknowledging the possibilities of success. It is crucial to possess a vision, maintain faith, and take action to achieve what we once aspired to. Cease hoping and manifest your desires!"

INSIGHT

Hope without motion becomes hesitation. Perspective shifts when your belief moves from wishing to walking. Vision grows when faith turns into action.

REFLECTION

- Where in your life are you waiting instead of creating?
- What small action could turn hope into momentum today?

EMOTIONAL STRENGTH

"Self-control is a manifestation of strength, and calmness represents mastery."

INSIGHT:

> Anyone can react. Leaders respond. Emotional discipline is the highest form of power.

REFLECTION:

- What triggers challenge your discipline?
- Where can you practice calm instead of control?

KNOWING SELF

"There are three exceedingly challenging endeavors: the forging of steel, the creation of a diamond, and the attainment of self-knowledge." — Benjamin Franklin, *Poor Richard's Almanack*

"The most challenging aspect of life is self-discovery." — Thales

INSIGHT:

> True understanding starts when ego ends. The journey inward is the hardest — and the most freeing.

- What truth about yourself have you avoided?
- Who are you becoming — by choice or by habit?

INTEGRITY IS WEALTH

"The true greatness of an individual lies not in the accumulation of wealth, but in their unwavering integrity and the positive impact they have on those around them." — Bob Marley

INSIGHT:

Money builds comfort — character builds legacy. The world remembers impact, not income.

REFLECTION:

- What do you want to be remembered for?
- Where can you serve instead of seek praise?

PRESENCE OVER TOMORROW

"Embrace the present moment fully, for tomorrow is uncertain. Reflect on what you wish to be remembered for if this were your final opportunity."

INSIGHT:

Tomorrow is a promise — not a guarantee. Your legacy is written in your today.

REFLECTION:

- Who needs your presence, not your plans?
- What action will matter five years from now?

BELIEF IS THE ENGINE

"Nobody believes more than I," — Kenny Emmett

INSIGHT:

When belief becomes identity, doubt cannot survive. Confidence creates power before proof arrives.

REFLECTION:

- What dream requires bigger belief?
- Where have you doubted yourself when you should have trusted your calling?

COMPARISON

"When you feel overwhelmed, do not give up. There will always be individuals facing greater challenges than you."

INSIGHT:

> An individual who possesses excessive knowledge for their own benefit becomes deaf to new information. They lose sight of their surroundings and become blind to reality.

> The moment we believe we know enough, we stop learning. Perspective shrinks when ego expands. Curiosity keeps us teachable.

REFLECTION:

- Where have you closed yourself off to learning?
- Who can humble your perspective?
- How can you become more curious?

HUMILITY

"Deaf to knowledge and sightlessness… Eventually, this individual loses their life because it becomes impossible for someone who knows everything to learn anything new."

INSIGHT:

It is impossible to truly understand someone's story until it is shared. Judging someone's character is foolish and inhumane. You are ignorant of the world I come from. Only God has the authority to judge me.:

Humility expands your perspective. Judgment is misdirected imagination. Stories reveal reality. Listening builds connection.

REFLECTION:

- Who have you judged prematurely?
- What story are you assuming without context?
- Where can humility open a door?

PRESENCE & LOSS

"Cherish each day with all your being. Tomorrow is never promised. Although tomorrow arrives, it is still today."

INSIGHT:

One moment, a person can be present, and the next, they are gone forever.

Perspective sharpens under loss. Awareness transforms urgency. Gratitude prevents regret.

REFLECTION:

- Who deserves more presence?
- What memory can you make today?
- Where are you rushing life?

ENDINGS & BEGINNINGS

"One moment, a person can be present, and the next, they are gone forever. It is always the one you least expect to meet death or perhaps, in the end it is truly life."

INSIGHT:

Choose your friends wisely, as they can become your greatest adversaries. Do not become overly comfortable and let your guard down prematurely before truly getting to know someone.

Perspective protects proximity. Not everyone deserves your inner circle. Awareness filters loyalty.

REFLECTION:

- Who sits too close without earning it?
- What boundary needs reinforcement?
- Who brings clarity, not chaos?

END-OF-CHAPTER CHALLENGE

For the next 5 days:

1. Notice your assumptions.
2. Ask one clarifying question daily.
3. Practice humility when tempted to judge.

Perspective deepens when curiosity replaces conclusion.

A.J.F.

Chapter 3

Mindset: The Architect of Your Outcomes

Knowledge, Humility & Growth

You can not fill a glass already pretending to be full. Insight requires space. Growth requires willingness. Wisdom begins where ego ends.

KNOWLEDGE & IGNORANCE

"An individual who possesses excessive knowledge for their own benefit becomes deaf to new information. They lose sight of their surroundings and become blind to reality."

INSIGHT:

> Deaf to knowledge and sightlessness… Eventually, this individual loses their life because it becomes impossible for someone who knows everything to learn anything new.

> Mindset collapses when pride replaces curiosity. The moment you believe you cannot learn, the world stops teaching. Growth is fed by humility.

REFLECTION:

- Where have you acted like you already knew?
- What lesson have you resisted because of ego?
- Who could teach you if you listened differently?

UNITY IN GROWTH

"Increased collaboration among individuals fosters collective growth and development. At this juncture, individuals attain a state of unity."

INSIGHT:

> Growth is contagious. When minds align with purpose, separation dissolves — unity becomes power.

REFLECTION:

- Who elevates your thinking when you are around them?
- Where can you collaborate rather than compete?

BE THE CHANGE FIRST

"Change resides within you, not in the ability to impose it upon others. Over time, change may or may not materialize. However, by transforming yourself, you have the potential to influence the situations and circumstances surrounding you."

INSIGHT:

> Change is not forced — it is modeled. The world responds to who you are, not who you demand others to be.

REFLECTION:

- What change are you waiting for others to make first?
- How can you embody the behavior you seek?

FEARLESS TRANSFORMATION

"To embody fearlessness is to become an indomitable force.

F - Fertilize / Focus / Fixate

E - Eat the frog

A - Annihilate the ANTs (Automatic Negative Thoughts)

R - Reticular — Stimulate your Reticular Activating System (Mind)

L - Love what is — Embrace Amor Fati

E - Energy Vampires — Release them

S - Stronger than ever — Utilize the Three W's (The What, The Who, & The When)

S - Stand Guard — At the threshold of your mind." – Pluck The F.U.D. by Ben Ward

INSIGHT:

> Fearlessness is not a feeling — it is a discipline. Each choice trains the mind toward expansion or retreat. Mastery begins where excuses end.

REFLECTION:

- What fear-based habit are you ready to dissolve today?
- Which inner discipline above do you most need right now?

POSITIVE MATH

"Positive times a Negative is equal to a Negative; Negative times a Negative is equal to a Negative; Positive times Positive equals a Positive."

Meaning:

"Positivity fosters positive alignment. Even on my most challenging days, I mentally prepared myself for a positive outlook."

INSIGHT:

Energy multiplies. Negativity always produces loss — positivity compounds into increase.

REFLECTION:

- Which energy are you multiplying today?
- Where do you allow negativity to drain your progress?

DAILY IMPROVEMENT

"Cultivate a positive mindset and consistently engage in self-improvement to foster a sense of well-being. Each day presents an opportunity for growth and enhancement."

INSIGHT:

Success is not a leap — it is a daily deposit. A better life is built brick by brick.

REFLECTION:

- What small habit can you add today that elevates your future?
- Where can you trade comfort for growth?

STRIVE FOR BETTER

"Strive to be a better version of yourself today, than you ever were yesterday or before."

INSIGHT:

Your only competition is the person in the mirror. Yesterday was training — today is execution.

REFLECTION:

- What version of you must evolve today?
- What behavior no longer belongs to who you are becoming?

SIMPLICITY WINS

"Overcoming challenges often requires simplicity, while pursuing the easier path can become more intricate."

INSIGHT:

Simplicity cuts noise. Complexity often hides fear. Most breakthroughs begin with clarity, not struggle.

REFLECTION:

- What solution are you overcomplicating?
- Where can you simplify your approach to succeed faster?

UNSTOPPABLE SPIRIT

"They can't stop me even if they stopped me." — Lil Wayne (lyric excerpt)

INSIGHT:

The strongest force in this world is a committed mind. Setbacks can only delay — they cannot deny.

REFLECTION:

- Where have you accepted defeat instead of delay?
- What proves you are built to outlast adversity?

KNOWLEDGE IS POWER

"Mastery of all is attainable through the cultivation of learning."

INSIGHT:

Knowledge is a lifelong discipline. The moment you stop learning, you start shrinking.

REFLECTION:

- What area of life deserves deeper study from you?
- Who or what can you learn from this week?

JUDGMENT

"It is impossible to truly understand someone's story until it is shared. Judging someone's character is foolish and inhumane. You are ignorant of the world I come from. Only God has the authority to judge me."

INSIGHT:

Cherish each day with all your being. Tomorrow is never promised. Although tomorrow arrives, it is still today.

Perspective grows with compassion. Judgment is often projection, not truth. Humility invites understanding; arrogance blocks empathy.

REFLECTION:

- Who have you misread?
- What story changed your opinion of someone?
- Where can empathy replace assumption?

ENVIRONMENTAL INFLUENCE

"To attain your desired outcome, you must be in the presence of what you seek. Surround yourself with individuals who possess the qualities you desire."

INSIGHT:

Birds of a feather flock together! Do you lead this flock or do you merely follow it? Take control and guide your flock towards a higher standard.

Your environment is louder than your intentions. Mindset is shaped by proximity. Who you sit beside eventually becomes who you become.

REFLECTION:

- Who drains your energy?
- Who elevates your thinking?
- Which room do you need to exit?

IGNORANCE & CONTROL

"Engaging in ignorance constitutes a self-imposed limitation. It is prudent to relinquish ignorance and embrace knowledge."

INSIGHT:

> While addressing ignorance may be necessary to uphold respect and character, it is paramount to maintain control and refrain from succumbing to ignorance.

> Responding with restraint is growth. Reaction protects ego; response protects purpose. Mindset chooses elevation over escalation.

REFLECTION:

- When did reacting cost you clarity?
- Where can you respond softer?
- What ignorance are you done entertaining?

OPINION INDEPENDENCE

"The opinions of others should not hold any significance for you."

INSIGHT:

> Recognize your true self and refrain from allowing anyone to alter your character based on their own perceptions. Cultivate self-love, and the validation of others will become inconsequential.

> Mindset's greatest prison is external validation. The more you seek approval, the more you lose identity. Confidence removes audience control.

REFLECTION:

- Whose opinion weighs too much?
- What part of you shrinks for acceptance?
- Where can you reclaim self-trust?

END-OF-CHAPTER CHALLENGE

For the next 7 days:

1. Practice active listening once daily.
2. Pause before reacting.
3. Spend time with someone wiser than you.
4. Notice when ego speaks louder than truth.

Growth begins when humility becomes habit.

A.J.F.

Chapter 4

Self-Regulation: Mastering Inner Chaos

Choices, Consequences & Accountability

Your future hides behind your decisions. Nothing changes until you take responsibility for who you are — and who you avoid becoming.

INTERNAL BATTLE

"Stress can lead to chaos and a distorted mindset. Maintain a clear and positive mindset, avoiding negativity at all costs. Positive actions have positive consequences, while negative actions have negative consequences. The first battle begins within ourselves. Without self-control, we lack a clear path to a fulfilled life."

INSIGHT:

As human beings, we are generally born with equal potential. We possess a unique way of thinking, creative ingenuity, and a sense of purpose. We instinctively recognize right from wrong. Therefore, it is our responsibility to maintain control over our human nature. We have both positive and negative traits, and discernment is essential in navigating these challenges.

Self-regulation is not suppression; it is mastery. Chaos outside is amplified by chaos inside. Peace is a product of boundaries, habits, and emotional clarity.

REFLECTION:

- Where is stress stealing clarity from you?
- Which emotion controls your reaction?
- What boundary protects your peace?

IGNORANCE REACTION

"Engaging in ignorance constitutes a self-imposed limitation. It is prudent to relinquish ignorance and embrace knowledge."

INSIGHT:

> While addressing ignorance may be necessary to uphold respect and character, it is paramount to maintain control and refrain from succumbing to ignorance.
>
> Reaction is a choice. A wise mind knows that not everything deserves energy. The loudest person rarely wins—clarity does.

REFLECTION:

- Who drains your energy most often?
- What topic triggers you easily?
- How can silence become strategy?

RESPOND, DON'T REACT

"Enhance your awareness of both reaction and response. Incorrect reactions and responses can significantly impact the outcome. By taking appropriate actions and responding with intention, you can increase the likelihood of favorable results. It is essential to recognize that not all situations require a reaction, and the decision to respond should be made carefully. Make wise decisions."

INSIGHT:

> Power is not in movement — it is in restraint. The strongest people are not those who strike first, but those who choose when not to.

REFLECTION:

- What reaction have you regretted before?
- Where can silence serve you more than a response?

PATIENCE + PRESENCE

"Exercise patience, but prioritize your time. Delaying for others who may not reciprocate, can squander valuable time that cannot be reclaimed. Time is of utmost importance."

INSIGHT:

> Patience is strength — but time is sacred. Protect your urgency the same way you protect your peace.

REFLECTION:

- Who or what drains your time without return?
- What deadline do you need to honor for yourself?

TRUTH REVEALS ITSELF

"Occasionally, unforeseen circumstances arise that catch us off guard. These moments can render us momentarily blind, but as time progresses, the truth will eventually emerge."

INSIGHT:

> Life exposes what emotion blinds. Trust time — clarity always comes, even when answers feel delayed.

REFLECTION:

- What truth has time revealed to you before?
- Where do you need to stop rushing the outcome?

LEARN IN MOTION

"You don't have to know anything to learn it; you just have to learn it to know it."

INSIGHT:

You grow by doing — not waiting. The door of mastery only opens once motion begins.

REFLECTION:

- What are you delaying because you feel unprepared?
- What is one step you can take before you "feel ready"?

WARRIOR DISCIPLINE

"A warrior is almost always hungry and thirsty during battle, but a warrior cannot take a break to do so!"

INSIGHT:

Comfort is a privilege, not a requirement for greatness. Purpose demands endurance — hunger builds champions.

REFLECTION:

- Where can you push through discomfort instead of pausing?
- What would the warrior version of you do today?

FINISH STRONG

"My aspiration is to allocate my final monetary resources on my final day of existence." — Patrick McBoogey

"I harbor no aversion to the concept of death. However, I am reluctant to be present during its occurrence." — Patrick McBoogey

INSIGHT:

Life is not measured by longevity — but by usage. Spend your time, energy, and gifts fully. Leave nothing unplayed.

REFLECTION:

- What dream deserves your full investment?
- Where in your life are you holding back resources or effort?

WISDOM IN TIMING

"Occasionally, certain knowledge may not necessitate verbalization or instruction until its true necessity becomes apparent."

INSIGHT:

Wisdom is knowing when to speak, and when silence is a strategy. Everything does not need to be shared — mastery includes timing.

REFLECTION:

- Where has withholding your thoughts served you?
- What wisdom are you still developing quietly?

CONSEQUENCE AWARENESS

Inputs Equals Outputs

"Life is contingent upon choices and intentions. The decisions we make in life shape our future. Before taking any action, it is crucial to consider the potential consequences. Making erroneous choices can lead to failure, while making sound decisions can pave the way for success."

INSIGHT:

A course will repeatedly take its place until you initiate a change. Redirect your path and remain vigilant for signs; otherwise, you will encounter the consequences.

Life repeats lessons until mastered. Accountability means seeing patterns instead of blaming circumstances. Change is a decision, not an accident.

REFLECTION:

- What cycle has repeated in your life?
- What haven't you changed yet?
- Where are consequences teaching you quietly?

RESPONSE WISDOM

"Enhance your awareness of both reaction and response. Incorrect reactions and responses can significantly impact the outcome."

INSIGHT:

> By taking appropriate actions and responding with intention, you can increase the likelihood of favorable results. It is essential to recognize that not all situations require a reaction, and the decision to respond should be made carefully. Make wise decisions.
>
> Power is found in pause. Emotion wants to speak first; wisdom lets silence filter truth. Self-regulation is not inaction—it is strategic action.

REFLECTION:

- Where can you pause instead of react?
- Who deserves a calmer response?
- What outcome do you want—really?

TIME OBLIGATION

"Exercise patience but prioritize your time. Delaying for others who may not reciprocate, can squander valuable time that cannot be reclaimed. Time is of utmost importance."

INSIGHT:

Occasionally, unforeseen circumstances arise that catch us off guard. These moments can render us momentarily blind, but as time progresses, the truth will eventually emerge.

Self-regulation includes time management. Time spent waiting on the wrong people becomes regret. Time spent training the right habits becomes legacy.

REFLECTION:

- Who has borrowed your time without return?
- What should no longer be delayed?
- How is time teaching you right now?

END-OF-CHAPTER CHALLENGE

For the next 5 days:

1. Delay your reaction by 5 seconds when triggered.
2. Name the emotion before responding.
3. Journal one repeated cycle you are ending.
4. Choose silence once a day.

Peace is not found—it is managed.

A.J.F.

Chapter 5

Values: Who Are You Without the Noise?

Environment, Associations & Leadership

You are not only influenced by your surroundings — you are sculpted by them. Leaders do not wait for permission; they raise the standard.

INFLUENCE CURRENCY

"Choose your friends wisely, as they can become your greatest adversaries. Do not become overly comfortable and let your guard down prematurely before truly getting to know someone."

INSIGHT:

Birds of a feather flock together! Do you lead this flock or do you merely follow it? Take control and guide your flock towards a higher standard. Just because you began your journey in financial hardship does not mean you must remain in that state indefinitely. I have guided my brothers and sisters towards financial stability. However, I cannot compel them to make positive choices, and if they choose not to, they are responsible for their own circumstances.

Your circle predicts your ceiling. Influence spreads silently. Comfort blinds discernment. Leadership is not declared —it is observed.

REFLECTION:

- Who in your circle drains or delays you?
- Who deserves closer access?
- Where are you following instead of guiding?

THE SWITCH OF INFLUENCE

"I aspire to be that pivotal switch, similar to the one that determines the direction of a train." — Devontae Baez

INSIGHT:

A single decision can redirect a life. Leadership often begins with the smallest internal shift — one deliberate pivot.

REFLECTION:

- Which tiny decision could change your trajectory?
- Whose life shifts when you choose higher?

DISCERN WHO YOU VOUCH FOR

"You may wish to advocate for others you are unfamiliar with. However, exercise caution before expressing positive opinions about individuals you lack knowledge of."

INSIGHT:

Discernment protects your character and reputation. Loyalty is honorable — but blind endorsement can cost credibility. Know who you elevate before you lend your name.

REFLECTION:

- Who do you cosign without truly knowing?
- How can you raise your standards for trust and association?

ENVIRONMENTAL OUTCOME

"To attain your desired outcome, you must be in the presence of what you seek. Surround yourself with individuals who possess the qualities you desire."

INSIGHT:

For instance, if you associate with individuals who are financially successful, you are more likely to achieve financial success as well. Conversely, if you surround yourself with individuals who are financially struggling, you are more likely to experience financial difficulties. The same principle applies to positive and negative environments, people, and conditions. In essence, act and embody the qualities you aspire to possess, as what is, already exists. Remember that like attracts like.

Proximity shapes identity. People are mirrors — some show you your growth, others show you your limits. Choose reflections that challenge you upward.

- Who reflects your potential?
- Who reflects your past?
- How can you select more intentionally?

ENVIRONMENT CREATES OUTCOME

"To attain your desired outcome, you must be in the presence of what you seek. Surround yourself with individuals who possess the qualities you desire. For instance, if you associate with individuals who are financially successful, you are more likely to achieve financial success as well. Conversely, if you surround yourself with individuals who are financially struggling, you are more likely to experience financial difficulties. The same principle applies to positive and negative environments, people, and conditions. In essence, act and embody the qualities you aspire to possess, as what is, already exists. Remember that like attracts like."

INSIGHT:

You do not rise alone — you rise with your circle. Your environment is shaping you even when you do not notice.

REFLECTION:

- Who do you admire that you need to be around more?
- Who drains your ambition and must be loved from distance?

CHOOSE YOUR FLOCK

"Birds of a feather flock together! Do you lead this flock or do you merely follow it? Take control and guide your flock towards a higher standard. Just because you began your journey in financial hardship does not mean you must remain in that state indefinitely. I have guided my brothers and sisters towards financial stability. However, I cannot compel them to make positive choices, and if they choose not to, they are responsible for their own circumstances."

INSIGHT:

> Leadership begins with example, not authority. You can show the way — but no one rises without choosing to.

REFLECTION:

- Are you leading or following right now?
- Who can grow with you — and who will not?

THE WEIGHT OF INFLUENCE

"The concept of owing someone can be both advantageous and burdensome… Patience is essential in such situations… remember that the money will eventually be received."

INSIGHT:

> Leverage and loyalty both carry weight. Trust wisely, but without fear — resources flow when your character earns them.

- Who has invested in you that deserves your gratitude?
- Where can you honor commitments more diligently?

PURPOSE OVER IMAGE

"Although I may occasionally adopt the label of a salesman, my primary role is to serve as a guide or source of assistance for others in achieving their desired outcomes, often without realizing they were seeking them."

INSIGHT:

Identity is earned through alignment, not labels. Service defines status — impact defines legacy.

REFLECTION:

- How do you want to genuinely serve others?
- Where can you replace "proving" with "providing?"

LOYALTY TO THE MISSION

"We are united in our efforts, and together, we shall achieve our goals."

INSIGHT:

The right team multiplies miracles. Unity is power — shared vision is momentum.

REFLECTION:

- Who is aligned with your purpose journey?
- What shared mission fuels your circle?

TRUE SELF LEADS

"Live authentically with yourself!" — Cat Vines

INSIGHT:

Authenticity is magnetic — imitation is exhausting. True leaders walk in self-truth.

REFLECTION:

- Where have you held back your real self?
- What truth do you need to stand in more boldly?

HUMILITY IN GROWTH

"I am actively engaged in my studies."

INSIGHT:

Students become masters because they never stop learning. Quiet work is sacred.

REFLECTION:

- What skill or discipline are you committed to improving?
- Where can you lower ego and raise curiosity?

JEALOUSY DIRECTIONS

"Jealousy can have two opposing effects: it can be a downfall for one individual while propelling another to success."

INSIGHT:

While we will always encounter detractors, it is crucial not to harbor animosity towards them. Instead, let their negativity serve as motivation to ascend to greater heights. Recognize that envious individuals solely desire your position, rather than pursuing their own aspirations. They will perpetually seek to surpass you.

Envy is misdirected admiration. Value-driven people allow jealousy to clarify priorities, not poison peace. Hate reveals desire.

REFLECTION:

- Who envies your growth? Why?
- How can you turn pressure into propulsion?
- Where can you release resentment?

SELF–WORTH ECONOMY

"Building genuine self-esteem requires individuals to first recognize and value their own worth. Delegating the responsibility of instilling self-worth to others can inadvertently lead to a lack of self-esteem."

INSIGHT:

We are given only one opportunity to live our lives. I am confident in my ability to make the most of this chance.

Self-worth becomes fragile when outsourced. Values build identity. When your worth is internally sourced, nothing external can subtract.

REFLECTION:

- Who have you depended on for validation?
- What belief elevates your worth internally?
- Where did your confidence originate?

DISPLAY & STEWARDSHIP

"We wholeheartedly support the concept of display, as it ensures that every individual will have the opportunity to witness it."

INSIGHT:

> However, it is crucial to recognize that only one individual will possess the key to unlocking the full potential of their display. Ultimately, the decision of who holds the key lies solely with the individual in question.
>
> Visibility without values becomes vanity. Stewardship is choosing who holds influence over your potential. Not everyone deserves a key.

REFLECTION:

- Who has keys to your potential?
- Should they?
- Who needs their key revoked?

END-OF-CHAPTER CHALLENGE

For the next 72 hours:

1. Audit your circle.
2. Set one boundary without apology.
3. Remove one negative influence quietly.
4. Elevate one peer through encouragement.

Leadership begins with who you choose.

A.J.F.

Chapter 6

Accountability: Facing the Mirror

Purpose, Faith & Calling

Purpose is not about comfort — it is about contribution. A calling whispers before it commands.

DIVINE TIMING

"Pursue the avenues that align with your knowledge and expertise, as they are likely to yield success."

INSIGHT:

> Consider a scenario where two individuals engage in excavation. One of the excavators discovers a diamond, prompting the other to cease digging and instead focus on uncovering the area behind the first excavator. However, the latter excavator was unaware that there were numerous diamonds situated significantly closer than he anticipated. Despite this oversight, he lacked confidence in his own plan. Therefore, it is crucial to follow your intuition and trust the plan devised by God. Trust in God's divine timing.

> Comparison steals destiny. Digging someone else's trench will not uncover your treasure. Faith trusts the unseen rhythm of timing.

REFLECTION:

- Where have you abandoned your progress to chase someone else's?
- What dream needs patience, not panic?
- How has timing protected you?

PRIDE'S DANGER

"Pride is an egoistic trait that can be our most significant flaw. Refrain from taking action driven by pride."

INSIGHT:

Instead, cultivate self-awareness and comprehend that you possess nothing to prove.

Pride builds castles around insecurity. Accountability tears them down to rebuild identity with honesty. Quiet confidence is louder than performance.

REFLECTION:

- When did pride block your growth?
- What insecurity is hiding underneath?
- Who are you without needing to prove?

SELF-ACCOUNTABILITY & FAITH

"Cultivating faith and taking action based on that faith is crucial. Embrace the limitless possibilities that life offers. By living in the present moment, you can align yourself with your true potential and thrive in this world."

INSIGHT:

> Accountability begins with faith — not just belief in something greater, but belief in your God-given capacity to grow. Growth requires presence, action, and discipline. The moment you take responsibility for who you are and where you are going, your life aligns with purpose.

REFLECTION:

- In what area of life do you need to take more responsibility?
- Where can you replace hesitation with faith-based action?
- What would happen if you trusted your purpose fully this week?

PURPOSE & SERVICE

"Although I may occasionally adopt the label of a salesman, my primary role is to serve as a guide or source of assistance for others in achieving their desired outcomes, often without realizing they were seeking them."

INSIGHT:

Service grounded in purpose is honorable work. You do not need a title — you need intent. True leaders guide without forcing and elevate others without announcing it.

REFLECTION:

- How do you serve others today without expecting recognition?
- Whose life can you quietly impact this week?
- Where can you show up and guide without announcing your presence?

PURPOSE & URGENCY

"Embrace each day as if it were your last. In doing so, live every second consistently and willingly taking action, to fulfill your purpose."

INSIGHT:

Purpose is not future tense — it is lived daily. One day you will run out of time. Discipline and urgency are the price of fulfillment.

REFLECTION:

- If today were your final day, what unfinished purpose would bother you?
- What delayed action can you commit to now?
- Where are you allowing procrastination to steal destiny?

UNITY & COLLECTIVE PURPOSE

"We are united in our efforts, and together, we shall achieve our goals."

INSIGHT:

Accountability also lives in community. Destiny grows where unity exists. A rising person rises others — and a weak circle weakens the strongest person.

REFLECTION:

- Who strengthens your mission? Who drains it?
- Where can collaboration accelerate growth?
- What is one way you can uplift your circle today?

PURPOSE WITH PRESSURE

"If your purpose does not evoke a profound emotional response or inspire you to transcend your limitations, then it is simply not significant enough. Your why has to shake your soul!"

INSIGHT:

Purpose is not comfortable — it confronts you, challenges you, stretches you. If your vision does not awaken emotion, it is not your highest assignment.

REFLECTION:

- Does your mission challenge you or comfort you?
- When did you last feel your purpose physically — not just think it?

PURPOSE THAT BREATHES

"If your purpose does not evoke a sense of awe and wonder, it may not be significant enough." — Unknown

INSIGHT:

Purpose should feel divine — something bigger than logic, louder than doubt, impossible to ignore.

REFLECTION:

- What dream feels too sacred to fully explain?
- Where is awe trying to lead you right now?

PERSONAL GROWTH COMMITMENT

"I am actively engaged in my studies."

INSIGHT:

> Self-accountability means staying a student — even when success comes. The most dangerous moment is when you believe you already know enough.

REFLECTION:

- What are you currently learning that is shaping your future?
- What discipline or skill must you develop next?
- Are you growing daily — or coasting comfortably?

STEPPING INTO FAITH

"May you find blessings in your endeavors, while blessing others and you will continue to be blessed!"

INSIGHT:

> Exercise patience but prioritize your time. Delaying for others who may not reciprocate can squander valuable time that cannot be reclaimed. Time is of utmost importance.

> Impact amplifies blessings. Accountability builds legacy. Faith without strategy becomes fantasy. Your calling holds a timeline—protect it.

REFLECTION:

- Who are you blessing just by being present?
- Where is reciprocity missing?
- How does purpose reorder your priorities?

VISIBLE ACTION

"Pay attention, and or attention will pay you. Always be aware of your surroundings, stay focused, and learn. Someone is always waiting and watching to take your place. Stay true to yourself and remain prepared!"

INSIGHT:

I understand your current situation. It is important to recognize that your past actions do not define your future. The choices you make moving forward will shape your destiny. You have the power to overcome this challenge. While some individuals may choose to distance themselves, those who genuinely care about you will remain steadfast in their support.

Preparation breeds opportunity. Accountability is proactive effort in hidden seasons. When you are trusted in private, you are elevated in public.

REFLECTION:

- What space do you need to prepare in quietly?
- Who is watching your growth silently?
- What action reveals intention?

LEGACY CALLING

"Every occurrence in life is not a mere coincidence; rather, it serves a specific purpose. Identify your purpose, and it will manifest itself to you."

INSIGHT:

> The commencement of my day significantly influences its end.

> "The future commences today, not tomorrow." — Pope John Paul II

> Purpose begins in daily decisions. Accountability is realizing your future self is watching your current choices. Legacy is built by repetition.

REFLECTION:

- Where have you delayed purpose?
- What habit honors tomorrows you?
- How can you begin before you feel ready?

END-OF-CHAPTER CHALLENGE

1. For the next 5 days:
2. Replace comparison with gratitude.
3. Serve someone anonymously.
4. Break one pride habit.
5. Act on purpose once per day.

Calling demands accountability.

A.J.F.

Chapter 7

Healing: Breaking Old Loops

Family, Roles & Legacy

Family carves character — not perfection, but preparation. Each role teaches responsibility.

FATHERHOOD BURDEN, MOTHERHOOD HEART, & Childhood Expectancy

"Fatherhood: The daily routine involves providing for the family's needs, including food and financial support. Despite the challenges, fathers are characterized by their unwavering determination and resilience."

"Motherhood: Motherhood entails nurturing and caring for the family, often neglecting personal well-being. Mothers require constant attention and support, yet they may not openly express their true needs, which include a balance of security and vulnerability."

"Childhood: Children are constantly guided and directed, yet they often feel compelled to exceed expectations and strive for excellence. Whatever they do, do not miss TLC."

INSIGHT:

> Healing acknowledges unseen sacrifice. The strongest nurturers often forget themselves. Legacy honors their invisible hours.

Family roles are often misunderstood from the outside. Healing begins when we recognize the silent weight each carries. Strength is service—not silence.

REFLECTION:

- Who carries weight you do not see?
- What support do you owe without being asked?
- How can you be present rather than perfect?
- Which caregiver needs gratitude from you?
- What did you learn through nurturing environments?
- How can you give back to the one who poured into you?

PRESSURE OF EXPECTATION

"The concept of owing someone can be both advantageous and burdensome. While it may initially seem stressful, it can also provide a sense of security and financial stability. By allowing someone to owe you money, you can benefit from the assurance that you will eventually receive your compensation."

INSIGHT:

This can be useful, particularly when you need funds for a specific purpose. Patience is essential in such situations, as the repayment process may take time. However, it is important to remember that the money will eventually be received, and that you can rely on the timely arrival of reimbursements.

Debt reveals dynamic. Expectations shape behavior. Healing
requires rebalancing emotional and relational transactions.

REFLECTION:

- Who are you indebted to emotionally?
- Where do you hold leverage, you no longer want?
- How can you forgive what can not be repaid?

HEALING THROUGH SERVICE

"Divine presence is ever-present. Maintain a high head and
concentrate on uplifting others. The joy and contentment we derive
from this act are invaluable compared to monetary success."

INSIGHT:

Healing grows through contribution. Helping others refines our
spirit and reveals our place in the world.

REFLECTION:

- Who can you uplift today — quietly, without reward?
- When has giving healed you more than receiving?

FACING FINISH LINES

"My aspiration is to allocate my final monetary resources on my final day of existence." — Patrick McBoogey

"I harbor no aversion to the concept of death. However, I am reluctant to be present during its occurrence." — Patrick McBoogey

INSIGHT:

> Healing deepens when we accept impermanence. Spend your time, gifts, and love fully—leave nothing unlived.

REFLECTION:

- What would you regret not finishing if this were your last year?
- Where are you saving effort when you should be spending it on purpose?

MOUNTAIN MINDSET

"CLIMB THE MOUNTAIN WITH ALL OF ITS OBSTACLES AND CHALLENGES IT MAY OFFER. YOU WILL ONE DAY REACH THE PEAK."

INSIGHT:

> Obstacles are not detours—they are the path. Healing builds altitude one honest step at a time.

REFLECTION:

- What "steep section" are you currently facing?
- What single step moves you upward today?

PRECISION & LEGACY

"Dravus: Comprehensive Interpretation. The name Dravus signifies an individual characterized by patience, meticulousness, and a preference for working in a precise and systematic manner, akin to disciplines such as mathematics, science, mechanics, computer science, or engineering."

INSIGHT:

Lasting healing is methodical. Patience and precision turn new habits into a family legacy.

REFLECTION:

- Where can you replace impulse with a system?
- Which patient practice will strengthen your lineage over time?

NEGATIVE LOOP BREAKING

"Progress is inevitable as long as we remain committed to moving forward."

INSIGHT:

Sometimes, the storm is necessary for us to shine.

Healing is not linear. Progress hides in pain. Storms uncover strength you forgot you had.

REFLECTION:

- What storm shaped you most?
- What loop ends when you choose differently?
- How is discomfort maturing you?

GENERATIONS & INFLUENCE

"When one is called home, another is sent out into the world."

INSIGHT:

It is akin to an octopus, with its arms extending in every direction. The feet are working tirelessly. Everyone I have connected with in the past, present, and future will reunite when we finally sit down for a definitive meeting. We will embark on a new journey together.

Legacy weaves across timelines. Healing honors those who came before and lifts those who come after. Influence echoes beyond breath.

REFLECTION:

- Who healed so you could climb?
- Who will rise because of your choices?
- How far does your ripple reach?

GRATITUDE & GRACE

"I am profoundly grateful for all that I possess, including the intangible aspects of life."

INSIGHT:

Gratitude and anxiety are incompatible emotions that coexist in a person's life. It is a conscious decision that we all make. As I become more aware of this, I am realizing that we possess the control and power to determine the direction our mindset takes at any given moment.

Gratitude is emotional medicine. It calms internal storms and softens generational narratives. Where anxiety closes, gratitude opens.

REFLECTION:

- What intangible gift changed your life?
- Where can gratitude reduce anxiety?
- Which internal storm needs peace today?

END-OF-CHAPTER CHALLENGE

For the next 72 hours:

1. Thank a family figure verbally.
2. Forgive one silent resentment.
3. Release ONE emotional debt.
4. Offer compassion without credit.

Legacy is lived by choice.

A.J.F.

Chapter 8

Purpose: Living Forward

Wealth, Work & Craft

Success is not purchased — it is prepared. Money follows value; value follows discipline; discipline follows purpose.

DAILY BRICK LAYING

"Lay a brick a day." - Nipsey Hussle (spoken)

INSIGHT:

> In my life, I am driven by a clear purpose. My objective is to meet the deadline at the end of my life. I recognize that achieving comfort will require me to endure discomfort. I am highly focused and determined, and I am willing to invest both time and effort to attain the desired results.

> Purpose is built brick by brick—not overnight. Small habits compound into identity. Discipline today becomes destiny tomorrow.

REFLECTION:

- What "brick" will you lay today?
- Where are you avoiding necessary discomfort?
- What habit defines your next level?

REWRITING REALITY THROUGH ACTION

"Before you can make life-changing money, you need to, first, change your life." — Micah Walls

INSIGHT:

Transformation starts with internal discipline—finances follow mindset, not the other way around.

REFLECTION:

- What behavior must change before your income can?
- Where are you waiting for results instead of creating them?

LIMITLESS DESIGN

"God did not create us with a governor; rather, God created us with limitless potential!" — Linnea Blizzard

INSIGHT:

Your ceiling is self-constructed. Remove internal limits and your external life expands to match.

REFLECTION:

- Where have you subconsciously limited yourself?
- What belief must you upgrade to access your next level?

ACCEPTANCE IS POWER

"The pursuit of more positive experiences can be perceived as a negative endeavor. Paradoxically, the acceptance of one's negative experiences can be considered a positive experience." — Mark Manson, inspired by Alan Watts

INSIGHT:

> Real growth does not eliminate storms — it learns to stand in them. Acceptance is not surrender; it is evolution.

REFLECTION:

- What discomfort are you resisting that you should be accepting?
- How can you grow from what you normally avoid?

REFINEMENT & MASTERY

"Mastery of all is attainable through the cultivation of learning."

"Self-control is a manifestation of strength, and calmness represents mastery."

INSIGHT:

> Purpose matures through discipline—mastery belongs to students of life, not shortcuts.

REFLECTION:

- Which skill will you commit to mastering?
- How can you practice calm strength daily?

THE SELF-DISCOVERY SUMMIT

"There are three exceedingly challenging endeavors: the forging of steel, the creation of a diamond, and the attainment of self-knowledge." — Benjamin Franklin, *Poor Richard's Almanack*

"The most challenging aspect of life is self-discovery." — Thales

INSIGHT:

Purpose is revealed on the other side of self-honesty. It will cost comfort, but reward clarity.

REFLECTION:

- What truth about yourself are you ready to face?
- In what ways have you evolved in the past year?

PURPOSE BEYOND POSSESSION

"The true greatness of an individual lies not in the accumulation of wealth, but in their unwavering integrity and the positive impact they have on those around them." — Bob Marley

INSIGHT:

> Purpose outlives possessions. Legacy is built on what you gave, not what you owned.

REFLECTION:

- How do you want to be remembered?
- Who benefits from your success besides you?

DIVINE ALIGNMENT & MOMENTUM

"Cultivating faith and taking action based on that faith is crucial. Embrace the limitless possibilities that life offers. By living in the present moment, you can align yourself with your true potential and thrive in this world."

INSIGHT:

> Purpose is spiritual alignment in motion—faith activates momentum and courage sustains it.

REFLECTION:

- Where do you need to lead with faith instead of fear?
- What action will prove your belief today?

MISSION MINDSET

"Although I may occasionally adopt the label of a salesman, my primary role is to serve as a guide or source of assistance for others in achieving their desired outcomes, often without realizing they were seeking them."

INSIGHT:

> Your calling is not what you sell—it is who you serve and who you lift in the process.

REFLECTION:

- Who do you exist to help?
- How do you deliver value beyond product or role?

UNITED ASCENT

"We are united in our efforts, and together, we shall achieve our goals."

INSIGHT:

> Purpose multiplies in community. Collaboration accelerates destiny; isolation delays it.

REFLECTION:

- Who must you align with to elevate faster?
- How can collaboration strengthen your impact?

SACRED TIME & DRIVE

"I am actively engaged in my studies."

INSIGHT:

Continuous self-investment guarantees continuous elevation. Study is worship for the ambitious soul.

REFLECTION:

- What are you studying to master your craft?
- What daily learning habit will secure your growth?

LIMIT BREAKING

"With unwavering determination, I am committed to surpassing my limitations and achieving extraordinary feats. I recognize that my own self-doubt can be my greatest obstacle, but I am resolute in my resolve to overcome it and embrace a life of limitless possibilities. Every day presents an extraordinary opportunity for growth and achievement. By consistently striving to surpass yesterday's accomplishments, we can reach new heights and transcend our perceived limitations. Through unwavering determination and daily perseverance, we can accumulate a wealth of experiences and accomplishments that far exceed our initial expectations."

INSIGHT:

> To achieve greatness, it is imperative to transcend one's own boundaries and push beyond perceived limitations.
>
> Your ceiling is self-imposed. Purpose demands confrontation with doubt. Growth happens where comfort ends.

REFLECTION:

- What limitation have you accepted as truth?
- When did doubt lie to you last?
- What boundary needs breaking this week?

NEXT LEVEL JOY

"To be joyous is to be a mad man in a world of ghosts" - Henry Miller, *Tropic of Capricorn*

"Upon mastering the art of aligning your soul, life will manifest with greater ease and fluidity. Action will become less arduous, and a profound sense of inner peace will envelop you, similar to that of a legate." - Kelsey Criswell

INSIGHT:

> Engage in meditation. Spend time in nature. Pursue your passions. Travel. Find joy in your daily activities. Embrace fearlessness!
>
> Purpose feels like madness to people without vision. Joy is a compass. Passion is a strategy. Peace is a product of alignment.

REFLECTION:

- Where do you feel most alive?
- What passion have you paused?
- What does joy teach you about calling?

WEALTH THROUGH VALUE

"Financial rewards are a consequence of adding value to the lives of others." - Paul McKenna

INSIGHT:

Seek fulfillment in relationships rather than solely in material possessions. Pursue personal growth and success will naturally follow.

Money follows meaning. Currency chases contribution. Purpose aligns prosperity with service—not consumption.

REFLECTION:

- Who can you add value to this week?
- Where do you confuse wealth with worth?
- What skill can you refine to serve more?

SUCCESS STANDARD

"Champions consistently go above and beyond their expectations, even when it involves making sacrifices." - James Kerr

INSIGHT:

> "As a collective, we must prioritize character development over mere reputation. Character represents our true selves, while reputation reflects the perceptions of others." – James Kerr

> Purpose is measured privately. Reputation is public performance; character is private consistency. Champions train unseen, then win publicly.

REFLECTION:

- Where are you relying on reputation?
- What character trait needs development?
- Who are you when no one watches?

SELF-TRANSFORMATION

"Kill yourself every day to give birth to the person you're destined to be."

INSIGHT:

> If you are not within your true self state of mind in the moment, take a mental break. Return with a refreshed and focused mindset (Back at 3,000%).
>
> Purpose requires micro-deaths—old habits, old identity, old environment. Reinvention is uncomfortable, but stagnation is fatal.

REFLECTION:

- What version of you must die for the next to rise?
- What belief must be buried?
- Who are you becoming intentionally?

END-OF-CHAPTER CHALLENGE

For the next 7 days:

1. Do one task outside your comfort zone.
2. Define a small habit with big impact.
3. Turn passion into discipline.
4. Speak your purpose out loud once daily.

Purpose pays those who commit.

A.J.F.

AFTERWORD

There is a moment in every journey when reflection becomes just as important as progress.

If you have made it to this page, you have done more than read — you have shown up for yourself.

You have chosen awareness over comfort, growth over stagnation, and truth over avoidance.

That alone already separates you from who you were when you began.

This book is not an ending.

It is a continuation — a reminder that becoming the best version of yourself isn't a destination, but a daily commitment. The words you have read were not meant to impress you; they were meant to awaken something within you. A voice. A realization. A shift.

If anything in these pages stayed with you… let it grow.

If something challenged you, … let it expand you.

If something resonated deeply, … honor it.

Life will continue to test your mindset, your discipline, your patience, and your vision.

But now you walk away with a sharpened sense of awareness, a clearer perspective, and a strengthened purpose.

You are no longer out of touch — you are becoming aligned.

As you step forward, remember this:

You do not rise all at once. You rise moment by moment. Decision by decision. Thought by thought.

You rise each time you choose intention over impulse, truth over ego, growth over comfort.

Your transformation does not require perfection — only presence.

Only honesty.

Only courage.

Thank you for walking through these chapters with me.

Thank you for allowing my words to meet your experiences.

And thank you for choosing growth, even when it was not easy.

Where you go next is entirely up to you — but I already know you are headed somewhere greater than you imagine.

Keep becoming.

Keep building.

Keep rising.

OUTSIDE QUOTE GALLERY

"Lay a brick a day."

— Nipsey Hussle (spoken)

Small, consistent effort compounds into identity,
discipline, and success.

"To be joyous is to be a mad man in a world of ghosts."

— Henry Miller, *Tropic of Capricorn*

True joy often looks crazy to people living on autopilot.

"Financial rewards are a consequence of adding value to the lives of others."

— Paul McKenna

Purpose-driven contribution attracts prosperity.

"Champions consistently go above and beyond their expectations, even when it involves making sacrifices."

— James Kerr

Excellence requires sacrifice few are willing to give.

"The strength of a team lies in the collective efforts of its members. Conversely, the strength of each member is derived from the team."

— Phil Jackson

Growth thrives in cooperation, not competition.

14. "You are the light of the world. A town built on a hill cannot be hidden."

* Neither do people light a lamp and put it under a bowl.

  Instead, they put it on its stand, and it gives light to everyone in the house.

* In the same way, let your light shine before others, that they may see your good deeds and glorify your Father in heaven." — Matthew 5:14–16 (KJV)

  Your actions are a candle—carry it with intention.

"The obstacle is the way!"

— Ryan Holiday

Obstacles are invitations for growth.

"There is no hill too steep for a stepper like me."

— Austin Rivers

Effort outlasts adversity.

"Proanoia — the belief that the universe is conspiring to do you good."

— The Definition

Where you place belief shapes experience.

"Your perspective on life holds the key to success."

— Betty White

A mindset of lightness unlocks resilience.

"Taking a wrong turn will allow you to see landscapes you have otherwise not seen."

— Rick Rubin, *The Creative Act: A Way of Being*

Mistakes carry secret blessings.

"Human beings often become what they believe themselves to be."

— Mahatma Gandhi (attributed)

Belief shapes capacity.

"The journey to success begins with small steps and the removal of obstacles."

— Confucius (attributed)

Progress favors the persistence.

"You simply cannot surpass the individual who never gives up."

— Babe Ruth

Consistency beats talent.

"If your why does not make you cry, it's not big enough!"

— Stacy Collins

Purpose requires emotional gravity.

"Ninety percent of self-improvement is knowing when to stop bullshitting yourself."

— (Uncredited aphorism — paraphrased)

Accountability begins internally.

Daily Quotes

Daily Quote 01

"Love unfolds — never force it. Time tells the truth that feelings alone cannot."

Daily Quote 02

"Assumptions are poison. Seek clarity or suffer in confusion."

Daily Quote 03

"Repetition without change is self-betrayal. Evolve or relive the same days."

Daily Quote 04

"When it feels impossible, remember — someone with less has overcome more."

Daily Quote 05

"The moment you know everything, you stop growing. Humility is the gate to wisdom."

Daily Quote 06

"You do not know someone's story. Honor humanity before judgment."

Daily Quote 07

"Tomorrow is a rumor. Today is all you have ever had."

Daily Quote 08

"Comfort creates blindness. Stay aware — loyalty wears masks before showing its face."

Daily Quote 09

"Stop hoping — start becoming. Faith + vision + action = reality."

Daily Quote 10

"To rise, stand in the rooms where greatness lives."

Daily Quote 11

"Lead your flock — don't just fly with them."

Daily Quote 12

"Your first battle is always with yourself — win there, win everywhere."

Daily Quote 13

"Knowledge grows the moment pride dies."

Daily Quote 14

"Self-love silences every outside voice."

Daily Quote 15

"Life will repeat the lesson until you change the student."

Daily Quote 16

"Stay alert — opportunity and danger both move quietly."

Daily Quote 17

"Envy reveals admiration in disguise — let it fuel you, not break you."

Daily Quote 18

"Trust God's timing — your blessing isn't late, it's preparing you."

Daily Quote 19

"Pride proves nothing — humility wins quietly."

Daily Quote 20

"Not every moment deserves your reaction — choose your response, choose your outcome."

Daily Quote 21

"Love people — but protect your access."

Daily Quote 22

"Patience is power — but time is priceless. Do not waste either."

Daily Quote 23

"Truth always rises — even when blindness comes first."

Daily Quote 24

"You do not have to know anything to learn it; you must learn it to know it. More in depth, you do not have to know it to begin — learning happens in motion."

Daily Quote 25

"Change yourself first — the world shifts after you do."

Daily Quote 26

"Fatherhood is sacrifice — strength without applause."

Daily Quote 27

"Motherhood is love disguised as endless responsibility — honor her."

Daily Quote 28

"Childhood is pressure to rise — make sure they feel love along the way."

Daily Quote 29

"Stay steady when people owe you — patience turns return into reward."

Daily Quote 30

"Negative energy multiplies itself — protect your peace first."

Daily Quote 31

"Don't chase comfort — growth demands discomfort."

Daily Quote 32

"Self-doubt is your loudest enemy — overcome it and become unstoppable."

Daily Quote 33

"Your purpose won't wait — meet it with urgency and faith."

Daily Quote 34

"Peace is a skill — earn it through discipline."

Daily Quote 35

"Rare minds don't fear standing alone — align your soul and your reality follows."

Daily Quote 36

"Every day is a brick — stack them with intention."

Daily Quote 37

"Purpose without action is just imagination."

Daily Quote 38

"Your level of success is closely correlated with your level of personal development. Success is an outcome of the person you become." — Jim Rohn

"Greatness is who you are — success is what follows."

Daily Quote 39

"True wealth is becoming — not owning."

Daily Quote 40

"Champions do more — especially when no one is watching."

Daily Quote 41

"Character is who you are — reputation is who they think you are. Protect the first."

Daily Quote 42

"Believe wholeheartedly that anything you set your mind to, can become a reality. Embrace the knowledge you acquire, and you will undoubtedly excel in your endeavors. Believe without limits — the world bends to conviction."

Daily Quote 43

"Stillness reveals truth — chaos cannot hide forever."

Daily Quote 44

"Your legacy lasts until the last time your name is spoken."

Daily Quote 45

"Choose your pain — discipline now or regret later."

Daily Quote 46

"If your desire is true, success is inevitable."

Daily Quote 47

"It is never too late or too early. It may simply not be the right time for you. Do not rush divine timing — but do not sleep on your calling."

Daily Quote 48

"Meticulousness is synonymous with intentionality. Precision is a mindset — intention in every move."

Daily Quote 49

"Fear is a test — walk through it and watch it bow."

Daily Quote 50

"If your 'why' does not shake your soul, it is not big enough."

Daily Quote 51

"Life rewards the ones who move — stagnation is silent surrender."

Daily Quote 52

"Sometimes the storm isn't against you — it's preparing you to shine."

Daily Quote 53

"Authenticity lies in embracing change and stepping out of your comfort zone. Stagnation is not the path to genuine fulfillment. Authenticity requires courage — comfort is the enemy of becoming."

Daily Quote 54

"Time is the real currency — spend it with intention."

Daily Quote 55

"Ambitious people struggle to rest until forced. This trait can be advantageous or detrimental — so balance it. And rest is not weakness — it is fuel. But do not abuse it."

Daily Quote 56

"In moments of chaos, tranquility will inevitably emerge. Chaos births clarity — storms settle, and truth rises."

Daily Quote 57

"Upon passing, one's true demise is not complete until the final day their name is uttered. Live so deeply you leave echoes after your name fades."

Daily Quote 58

"Endure now — so your future self can live free."

Daily Quote 59

"Desire fuels destiny — necessity alone rarely builds greatness."

Daily Quote 60

"Purpose grows louder the more you honor it — keep showing up."

Daily Quote 61

"Faith isn't passive — it's action disguised as trust."

Daily Quote 62

"When God calls you forward, comfort becomes the enemy."

Daily Quote 63

"You only lose when you stop — persistence destroys defeat."

Daily Quote 64

"Life presents challenges, but ease is a byproduct of effort. Remember that ease is earned — struggle is the admission price."

Daily Quote 65

"Leaders rise because they lift others first."

Daily Quote 66

"Life presents challenges, but ease is a byproduct of effort."

Daily Quote 67

"Your past explains you — not defines you."

Daily Quote 68

"When you possess faith and determination, you realize everything is under divine control. Faith means stepping when the ground is not visible."

Daily Quote 69

"Your light isn't yours to hide — shine so others can see the way."

Matthew 5:14 — "Let your light shine before others."

Daily Quote 70

"Service is the highest sales pitch — help first, value follows."

Daily Quote 71

"Individuals may not fully understand my identity until they meet me in person. Identity is discovered, not assigned — live who you are becoming."

Daily Quote 72

"Self-worth is built internally — not borrowed from applause."

Daily Quote 73

"Life gives you one chance — honor it by living all the way in."

Daily Quote 74

"Taking a wrong turn allows you to see landscapes otherwise unseen" — The Creative Act: A Way of Being Rick Rubin

"Wrong turns reveal hidden destinations — nothing is wasted."

Daily Quote 75

"Gratitude lifts anxiety — both cannot live in the same room."

Daily Quote 76

"Find humor in daily experiences — do not take life too seriously. This power can prove invaluable in challenging situations" — Betty White

"Live lightly — seriousness suffocates the miracle of living."

Daily Quote 77

"Purpose requires urgency — time never refunds regret."

Daily Quote 78

"Cultivate wisdom, not age. Embrace your imagination and maintain a youthful outlook. Wisdom is not age — it is curiosity practiced daily."

Daily Quote 79

"If I believe I can achieve, the ability will come" — Mahatma Gandhi

"Belief creates ability — long before ability proves belief."

Daily Quote 80

"Take control of your mind by actively seeking knowledge and personal growth. Striking a balance between positivity & avoiding negativity is crucial. Your mind obeys what you feed it — direct it or default to noise."

Daily Quote 81

"The journey to success begins with small steps and the removing of obstacles." — Confucius

"Success begins at the first step — not the finish line."

Daily Quote 82

"Income follows impact — build value, not vanity."

Daily Quote 83

"Relationships water your becoming — choose gardens, not weeds."

Daily Quote 84

"Champions work when others rest — excellence isn't convenient."

Daily Quote 85

"Character is truth — reputation is only rumor."

Daily Quote 86

"Become the person success requires — then success arrives."

Daily Quote 87

"To grow, step beyond comfort — authenticity lives outside familiar walls."

Daily Quote 88

"The value of time becomes apparent only when it has passed"
— Austin Rivers

"Time is priceless — honor it before it escapes your memory."

Daily Quote 89

"Ambition needs discipline — speed without control crashes."

Daily Quote 90

"Chaos tests you — and peace finds you on the other side."

Daily Quote 91

"Legacy lives beyond breath — you die twice, so live fully now."

Daily Quote 92

"Pain is inevitable — control your own suffering by choosing discipline. Choose discipline now or regret later — pain is unavoidable, but purpose chooses its form."

Daily Quote 93

"If you do it out of necessity it won't work — do it out of desire" — Sawyer Pickens

"Move from need, to desire — what's forced fails, what's fueled flourishes."

Daily Quote 94

The Just Do Motto!

"Embrace your purpose and pursue your goals with unwavering determination. Do not wait for confidence — build it by moving anyway."

Daily Quote 95

"Cultivate faith and take action — limitless potential unfolds in the present. Faith is not hoping — it is knowing while walking forward."

Daily Quote 96

"Live with unwavering determination toward your purpose. Purpose does not whisper — it roars when you finally listen."

Daily Quote 97

"Discomfort feeds destiny — comfort protects average."

Daily Quote 98

"Gratitude dissolves anxiety — both cannot live in the same breath."

Daily Quote 99

"Kill who you were — to become who you're here to be."

Daily Quote 100

"The future commences today, not tomorrow." — Pope John Paul II

"Start today — tomorrow is a myth disguised as a promise."

Daily Quote 101

"Self-mastery is the highest strength — calm is the highest power."

Daily Quote 102

"You cannot beat the one who refuses to quit."

Daily Quote 103

"A leap of faith builds the bridge while you are crossing it. Embrace the leap of faith!"

Daily Quote 104

"Storms reveal your shine — embrace them, don't fear them."

Daily Quote 105

"Greatness is repetition — brick by brick, belief by belief."

 REFLECTION & JOURNAL WORKBOOK

✨ **"Awareness without reflection is blindness. Reflection without action is stagnation."**

This workbook is your mirror — the place where insight becomes transformation.

Each prompt is a moment of self-conversation between your truth and your potential.

Pause. Breathe. Reflect. Write with purpose.

CHAPTER 1 — AWARENESS

"You cannot change what you refuse to notice."

INSIGHT REMINDER:

Awareness awakens truth. You cannot change what you refuse to notice.

REFLECTION PROMPTS:

- What truth about yourself has recently come to light?
- Which distractions keep you from seeing reality clearly?
- How does silence help you understand yourself better?
- What moment made you "wake up" to a deeper truth?

Write your reflections below:

____

____

____

____

____

____

____

⬛ "Awareness begins the moment you decide to be honest with yourself."

CHAPTER 2 —PERSPECTIVE

"When you change the way you look at things, the things you look at change." — Wayne Dyer

INSIGHT REMINDER:

Your perception shapes your reality. Shift your view, shift your world.

REFLECTION PROMPTS:

- What old belief needs to be challenged?
- When have you misjudged a situation because of assumption?
- How has your pain taught you to see differently?
- In what ways does gratitude reframe your perspective?

Write your reflections below:

____

____

____

____

🌑 "Your eyes see what your mind believes."

CHAPTER 3 — MINDSET

"Master your mind, or it will master you."

INSIGHT REMINDER:

Your mindset builds your life — one thought, one choice, one day at a time.

REFLECTION PROMPTS:

- What mental habit has the most power over your emotions?
- How can you turn self-doubt into discipline?
- Who inspires you to think bigger?
- What do you need to start believing about yourself?

Write your reflections below:

____

____

____

____

____

____

💬 "The moment you decide, the universe aligns."

CHAPTER 4 — SELF-REGULATION

"Discipline is the bridge between goals and accomplishment." — Jim Rohn

INSIGHT REMINDER:

Discipline is freedom in disguise. Control your reactions — command your path.

REFLECTION PROMPTS:

- What situations trigger the "worst" version of you?
- How can you pause before reacting?
- What daily rituals keep you grounded?
- How does emotional mastery influence your relationships?

Write your reflections below:

____

____

____

____

____

____

🕯️ "Your peace is power — protect it like your life depends on it."

CHAPTER 5 — VALUES

"You become what you tolerate."

INSIGHT REMINDER:

You attract what you align with. Protect your energy and guard your circle.

REFLECTION PROMPTS:

- Who truly reflects your values — and who does not?
- What does loyalty mean to you now?
- Where have you compromised your standards?
- How can you lead through example, not explanation?

Write your reflections below:

____

____

____

____

____

____

____

🖋 "Be so rooted in your values that storms only shake your leaves."

CHAPTER 6 — ACCOUNTABILITY

"The price of greatness is responsibility."

— Winston Churchill

INSIGHT REMINDER:

Responsibility is the foundation of personal power.

REFLECTION PROMPTS:

- What decision are you currently avoiding?
- Who deserves your apology — or forgiveness?
- What pattern do you need to take full ownership of?
- What would your life look like if you removed all excuses?

Write your reflections below:

____

____

____

____

⚖️ "Accountability isn't punishment — it's progress."

CHAPTER 7 — HEALING

"Healing is not about becoming who you were;
it's about becoming who you're meant to be."

INSIGHT REMINDER:

Healing is not becoming who you were — it is becoming who you are meant to be.

REFLECTION PROMPTS:

- What wound still seeks your attention?
- What do you gain by releasing the past?
- How do you know when healing has begun?
- Who have you become since your last heartbreak?

Write your reflections below:

____

____

____

____

____

____

💧 "Healing is messy — but it's yours."

CHAPTER 8 — PURPOSE

"Don't ask what the world needs.
Ask what makes you come alive and go do it."
— Howard Thurman

INSIGHT REMINDER:

Purpose is not found — it is remembered. You've had it within all along.

REFLECTION PROMPTS:

- What drives your heart the most?
- What would you do even if you were never paid for it?
- How can you serve others through your gifts?
- What legacy will your story leave behind?

Write your reflections below:

____

____

____

____

____

"Purpose is a whisper that becomes a roar when you're ready to listen."

ACKNOWLEDGMENTS

To those who have walked beside me, crossed paths with me, challenged me, or inspired me — this book carries pieces of every one of you.

To the reader holding these pages:

You are the reason this book breathes.

Your willingness to grow, to question, to heal, and to rise is the highest honor a writer could receive. Thank you — sincerely.

To my family, my friends, and all the souls who have touched my journey, whether through a conversation, a passing moment, or a silent act of kindness — your presence has shaped me more than you may ever know. Even strangers have left fingerprints on my evolution.

I thank the many versions of myself — the broken ones, the hopeful ones, the lost ones, and the unshakeable ones.

Each version walked me here.

Each version refused to quit.

And for that, I am grateful.

To my mother — your love is a quiet strength that carried me farther than you realize.

To my father — your sacrifices were lessons dressed as burdens, teaching me how to provide, endure, and rise.

To my grandparents — your drive and discipline planted seeds I am
still harvesting.

To those who allowed me to be vulnerable and reciprocated with the
same level of transparency — you helped me grow in ways I cannot
measure. Thank you — you know who you are.

And above all, to God —

the One who guided me through confusion, anchored me in purpose,
and reshaped me through fire.

Your timing, Your tests, and Your grace brought me to the very place
this book was meant to be written.

If your name is not spoken here, know this:

gratitude does not need ink to exist.

Some of you contributed in whispers, in shadows, in moments so
subtle you may not even remember them.

But I do.

And you are seen.

To those credited throughout these pages — thank you for lending me
your perspectives, your truths, and your light.

More of you will surely appear as new volumes are born.

To all who helped me become —

thank you.

About the Author

Anthony J. Fryer, widely known as Smiley, is a voice for growth, reflection, and self-awareness.

Born from struggle and transformation, his perspective on life was shaped through challenges that tested not just his strength, but his sense of purpose.

Raised in an environment that taught survival before peace, Anthony's journey led him through moments of pain, healing, and rediscovery. In 2019, during a pivotal period of isolation, he began to write—not to impress, but to express.

Each word became a reflection of his truth, his lessons, and his deep belief that we all have the capacity to rise beyond what we have been through.

Today, Anthony continues to inspire others to reframe their reality — reminding them that awareness, mindset, and purpose are the foundations of transformation. Through his writing, speaking, and influence, he encourages individuals to realize that they are never too late, too lost, or too broken to begin again.

When he is not writing, he is observing life — learning, connecting, and pushing forward with gratitude, intention, and unshakable faith.

"It's not about being perfect — it's about being present."

— Anthony J. Fryer largely known as Smiley

PREVIEW | WHAT COMES NEXT

What comes next is not comfort. It is confrontation.

If Volume I cracked open the door, Volume II tears it off the hinges.

The next chapter of this journey dives into the places we avoid —

the shadows where our truth waits, watching us return to the same lessons we swore we had already mastered.

In the pages ahead, you will face the parts of yourself that whisper

when you are alone…

the patterns you pretend you have outgrown…

and the voice you silence because you are afraid it might be right.

In Volume II, the questions get sharper, the insights get heavier, and the reflections cut closer to the bone.

This is growth without a mask.

Healing without a hiding place.

Awakening without permission.

If you felt something shift in this volume, prepare for the moment everything inside you turns.

You have opened the door.

Now step into what is waiting.

Connect with the Author

If this book spoke to you — if it sparked reflection, healing, or purpose — I would love to hear from you.

Your journey matters, and every shared story reminds us that growth is universal.

Stay connected for future releases, reflections, and upcoming volumes of What We Fail To Realize.

Follow & Connect:

Instagram: @_360LowkeySmilez

                    @Smilez.Hazely.Ent.LLC360

Facebook: Low Key

Website: Coming Soon…

Continue to walk with awareness, live with intention, and move with purpose. The journey does not end here — it evolves with you.

— Anthony J. Fryer largely known as Smiley